BRITAIN SINCE 1948

Working Life

Neil Champion

WAYLAND

First published in 2008 by Wayland

Wayland
338 Euston Road
London NW1 3BH

Wayland Australia
Level 17/207 Kent Street
Sydney, NSW 2000

Editor: Katie Powell
Designer: Phipps Design

British Library Cataloguing in Publication Data

Champion, Neil
    Working life. - (Britain since 1948)
    1. Occupations - Great Britain - History - 20th century - Juvenile literature
    2. Social change - Great Britain - History - 20th century - Juvenile literature
    3. Great Britain - Social conditions - 20th century - Juvenile literature
    I. Title
    331.7'00941'09045

ISBN: 978 0 7502 5375 8

Printed in China

Wayland is a division of Hachette Children's Books,
an Hachette Livre UK company
www.hachettelivre.co.uk

Picture acknowledgements: Advertising Archives: 18, 22, AP/Topham: 14
Tim Beddow/Science Photo Library: 17, Bettmann/Corbis: 11, Ashley
Cooper/Corbis: 25, Mary Evans PL/Alamy: 12, Mary Evans PL: 16, 20
John Frost Newspaper Archive: 19, Tom Grill/Corbis: front cover bl, 27, 29
Hulton Archive/Getty Images: front cover br,8, Hulton-Deutsch/Corbis: 4, 5, 6,
9, Image State/Alamy: 13, Betrand Langlois/AFP/Getty Images: 26, Museum
of London/HIP/Topfoto: 10, Andreas Pollok/Digital Vision/Getty Images: 28.
Popperfoto: 24, Reuters/Corbis: 21, Dennis Stone/Rex Features: 23.
Wayland Picture Library: 7, 15

Contents

Words in **bold** can be found in the glossary.

Britain in 1948

The working lives of people in 1948 were very different from those of most people in Britain today. There were far fewer of us – 47 million as opposed to 60 million today. Out of those in work, very few were women – only a third had any form of paid employment. Most jobs for women were in domestic work. The majority of men worked manually – in factories or in industry, on the railways, in the Post Office or in agriculture. The average wage was just £325 a year.

Another World

Britain was emerging from the horrors of the Second World War. The British **economy** was weak and **manufacturing** was yet to pick up. **Rationing** was in place in 1948 and stayed until 1954, as food, fuel and energy were still in short supply. This was '**Austerity Britain**'.

Voices from history

'I came to London from Jamaica on 21st June 1948 on the Windrush. I came because I wanted to gain more knowledge towards the making of clothes. First of all I had to find somewhere to live... We were put up in a deep shelter in Clapham. "What work do you do?" I said, "I'm a tailor." He said, "We haven't got any jobs for tailors right now, would you mind working in a mine?" I said, "Oh, no sir." I was anxious to get something to do. I'd do anything rather than steal.'

Clifford Fullerton speaking in an extract from *The Motherland Calls*, the Ethnic Communities Oral History Project, 1989.

TIMELINE

1948	The first modern computer comes in to use
1948	The railways in Britain are **nationalised**
1948	The Olympic Games are held in London. Known as the 'Austerity Games'
1948	The Labour government creates the Welfare State and the National Health Service (NHS)
1948	The British workforce is made up of 20.5 million people – 6 million of those are women

Empire Windrush • These men have come to Britain from Jamaica aboard the ship, Empire Windrush. The year is 1948 and 492 immigrants docked in London.

However, unemployment was very low. Less than 2% of men were out of work, compared with over 7% in the late 1970s and 12% in the late 1990s. Most of Britain's energy came from coal. Nuclear power had been discovered but no nuclear power stations had yet been built.

Change Afoot

In 1948, an event occurred that would change the face of Britain in many ways in the years to come, yet at the time it went almost unnoticed by most people. Britain still had a large empire that consisted of **colonies** overseas.

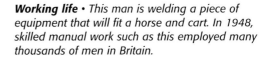

Working life • *This man is welding a piece of equipment that will fit a horse and cart. In 1948, skilled manual work such as this employed many thousands of men in Britain.*

In June 1948, a ship called the *Empire Windrush* brought 492 people from British colonies in the Caribbean and docked in London. It signalled the start of multicultural Britain. These were men and women from Jamaica and Trinidad. Work was plentiful in Britain at this time and they soon found jobs, mostly in manual jobs such as mining, on the railways, in the Post Office or in the Salvation Army, as the man in our panel eventually did.

Life on the Land

Working on the land is one of the oldest jobs in the world. However, this ancient occupation was undergoing huge changes in post war Britain. In 1948, there were about three quarters of a million people in Britain working on the land, involved in the production of food – dairy products, meat, cereals, vegetables and fruit. These people ranged from landowners and **tenant farmers** to hired unskilled agricultural workers. Agriculture was still an important industry, worth over £640 million. While some of the work was still done by hand – for example, haymaking and threshing – people were slowly being replaced by machinery.

TIMELINE

1948	5% of the working population work in agriculture	
1961	4% of the working population work in agriculture	
1981	2% of the working population work in agriculture	
1998	The farming workforce is at 312,000	
2006	Agriculture contributes £5.5 billion to the British economy	
2006	Average income for a farm in Britain is £20,600	

▲

Working the land · *This photograph was taken in Scotland in 1955. It shows farm workers reaping the crop of grain with a scythe, a large cutting blade on the end of a long pole. This was hard manual labour.*

Voices from history

'I do actually remember the first combine harvester that came into this village. It was in the early years after the war, and Mr Ferreira, who had been doing contract work – giving that sort of service in the area throughout the war years – had a combine to trial. Whether or not it came on a trial or hire basis, I've no idea, but I remember him taking it off to try, and my grandfather commenting, "Aye those things maybe alright in Canada, but they're not any good in this country." But, of course, these things all have to be adapted and time changes everything, doesn't it?... On our farm we milked up to twenty-five to twenty-eight cows, that sort of figure, and it was all done by hand until after the war, when the milking machines were introduced. There were one or two people, possibly two in the village, who had them from the beginning of the war, but certainly not more.'

Leslie Derrick, a farmer, interviewed for *Agriculture on the Nottinghamshire Wolds* website in 2001.

▲
Machines take over • *A combine harvester taking in the wheat. In a fraction of the time this machine can do the work that was once done by dozens of farm labourers.*

Farming over the Decades

However, machines such as tractors, milking machines and combine harvesters, were being introduced from the 1940s onwards, though it took several decades for most farms in Britain to become fully mechanised.

Oxen were still used to pull ploughs on some farms in the 1940s as well as horses. But by the 1960s, these were becoming rarer sights. As a consequence of this increasing mechanisation, the number of people employed on the land was to decline rapidly over the decades as machines took on more of the work. Fifty years later, just over 300,000 people worked on farms, well under half that of 1948. Another major change was that many small farms were being bought by larger landowners. The face of British farming changed in this way as agriculture became increasingly industrial on a scale to compete with farmers in other countries.

Workplace Winners and Losers

Since 1948, the work that people do in Britain has changed considerably. There were many industries, as well as farming, that were set to change and some, such as coal mining, have virtually disappeared altogether.

However, many jobs that provide work today, did not exist in 1948. There were no software engineers as there was no computer industry. Today, the computer industry employs many thousands of people. The broad movement was from manual and unskilled employment to skilled office workers and technicians. Some jobs declined and some have become increasingly important in the modern world.

Mining and Heavy Industries

Coal mining employed nearly 800,000 people in 1948 and produced 200 million tons of coal in that year. Fifty years later, the industry's workforce had shrunk to 2% of the 1948 total. The industry declined when it became cheaper to **import** coal rather than mine our own. This was due to the relatively high wages of miners compared with those working in other countries. Also, coal was becoming increasingly more expensive to extract as miners had to go deeper and deeper underground.

Underground • *A coal miner in 1950s Britain putting his lamp away after a day's work underground at the coalface. At about this time, almost 700,000 people worked in this industry.*

▼

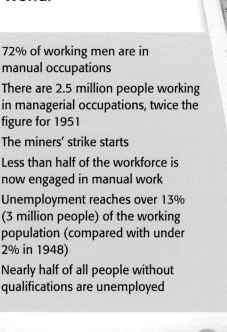

TIMELINE

1951	72% of working men are in manual occupations
1971	There are 2.5 million people working in managerial occupations, twice the figure for 1951
1972	The miners' strike starts
1981	Less than half of the workforce is now engaged in manual work
1984	Unemployment reaches over 13% (3 million people) of the working population (compared with under 2% in 1948)
2005	Nearly half of all people without qualifications are unemployed

Festival of Britain • *A photograph of the main site of the Festival of Britain – the South Bank near Waterloo Station in London. The Festival was held in 1951 and aimed to show post war progress in society and industry.*

In the 1950s, oil and its main by-product, petrol, overtook coal as the main source of energy. Coal-powered engines were replaced with diesel and petrol engines, for example. The first nuclear power station in Britain was switched on in October 1956. Coal was no longer the important product it had once been. By the early 1990s, there was only a fraction of the mines left open and only 17,000 people employed to work in them.

Other heavy and manual industries that have declined over the decades include steel production and car production. These industries saw a drop in the number of people working in them and in their economic importance in Britain. In 1965, nearly all the cars bought in Britain were also made here. In 1980, less than half the cars bought were made in Britain. Countries like Japan and Germany had overtaken Britain in car production.

The Rising Professions

Meanwhile, the service industries were on the rise. Manual work was becoming less necessary and education was becoming more important. In the 1950s, just over one in ten people worked in a professional capacity. By the mid 1960s this had changed. Over half the workforce had jobs in the service industries, as office workers, with those working in manual jobs in sharp decline. In the 1970s, with the rise of computers and the importance of the service industries this change became more obvious. By the 1990s, two thirds of the working population had office jobs.

Women and the Workplace

Another aspect of life in Britain that was to alter was the role of women. In 1948, most women still ran the household, did the cleaning and cooking and brought up their children. Husbands and sons went out to work, in an age where manual jobs were plentiful and there was almost full employment.

Seeds of Change

However the seeds of change had been sown a few years earlier during the Second World War. Between 1939 and 1945, many men were in the army fighting abroad. Women were drafted onto farms and into factories to keep the nation fed and industry ticking over. When the soldiers came home, women continued to hold a place in the workforce.

By the 1950s, women were beginning to enter the workplace in larger numbers than ever before. Many went into the lower paid jobs (such as cleaning, catering, caring and clerical work) and part-time employment, but this too was to change over time. Between the late 1940s and the 1990s, the number of working men has remained about the same (almost 15 million), but the number of women working has more than doubled – up from around six million to over 12 million.

Women at work in the 1950s • *A photograph of women working as typists in an office in London in the 1950s.*

TIMELINE

1948	Six million women are at work either full-time or part-time
1951	35% of women aged 16 or over work either full-time or part-time
1979	Margaret Thatcher becomes the first female British Prime Minister
1993	12 million women in the workplace
2006	75% of working women work in five main areas – cleaning, catering, health care, cashiering and clerical work.

Equal Pay

About three quarters of all women working today are still in lower paid professions. The Equal Pay Act of 1970 was brought in to give women better pay and opportunities in the workplace. However, it has been estimated that it will take 200 years from now for there to be as many women Members of Parliament (MPs) in parliament as there are male MPs at the current rate of change.

▲ **Women in politics** • *Conservative leader Margaret Thatcher and her husband Denis standing outside 10 Downing Street. Margaret Thatcher became the first British female Prime Minister in 1979.*

CHANGING TIMES

Today, on average, for every £10 that a man earns at work, a woman will only earn £8.20. This is even lower in part-time occupations. For every £10 that a man earns working part-time, a woman will earn £6.

In 2004, less than one MP out of five was a woman. In top jobs in management, less than one third are women. Just over one in ten women are directors in companies in Britain today. There is still a long way to go before women are truly on an equal footing with men, but the opportunities have changed massively since 1948.

Education and the Workplace

One of the most significant changes in the employment industry between 1948 and today has been the need for people to have more school, college or university qualifications. This reflects the change from manual jobs to office jobs that often require professional qualifications. Britain is no longer primarily an industrial and farming nation but one that places high importance on the education of its workforce.

A classroom scene from the 1950s •
Lessons in the 1950s were very different from lessons today. Boys would sit in orderly rows and a teacher would often dictate to them.

Work in the Service Industry

Today, about two thirds of all employed people work in the service sector, in offices, using computer, numeracy and literacy skills. There is a direct link between the level of education and level of income in today's society.

It is estimated that 10% extra income can be earned for each year in education after the age of 16. In the 1950s and 1960s, there were eight million jobs for unskilled manual workers. Today, there is half that number and it is falling all the time.

TIMELINE

1954-55 There are 82,000 students at university across Britain

1961-2 14,276 full-time staff at British universities

1979-80 There are just over 185,000 men and 107,000 women in higher education in Britain

1984 42,000 full-time staff at British universities

2005 Nearly half of all people without qualifications are unemployed compared with just over one in ten of those with a degree or similar qualification

Science in the twenty-first century • *Today's lessons are much more interactive. These students are studying human anatomy in a biology class, in a well equipped school classroom.*

Higher Education

In the global economy of the twenty-first century, post-compulsory education has become very important. It is often a necessary requirement for getting a job. In the 1960s, polytechnics were created and traditional universities were expanded to cater for a growing demand from students. In 1980, about 13% of school leavers went on to take a place in higher education. By 2000, this had risen to 33%. The government has a target of 50% of all school leavers entering higher education by 2010.

CHANGING TIMES

Another aspect of working life today, is that many people choose to change careers far more often than they ever could in the past. In the 1950s, the majority of people stayed in one profession all their working lives. Today, there is a lot more choice and that includes going back to being a student at any age.

Accountants, lawyers, editors, teachers, lecturers, doctors and consultants – these are just a few of the many jobs that require some form of higher education.

The Changing Face of Industrial Britain

Britain had declined as an industrial country by the end of the twentieth century. Big industries such as ship building, coal mining and car making lost out to companies in other countries. Education and qualifications were replacing labouring skills. However, some industries, such as the Post Office, survived by changing with the times and remaining competitive.

The Post Office

As communication between towns and cities at home and abroad has become increasingly important, so the role of the Post Office has grown. Today, there are about 21 billion items of post sent each year – on average a staggering 87 million a day to 27 million addresses.

Voices from history

'From Gigha I can well remember pairs of rabbits going off with just a band around the middle of the rabbits with the address on and that was it… Hens would go off in the post and they'd just have their legs tied and a label tied to their legs…'

The Post Office serves the most remote parts of the British Isles. Here the postmaster in the Isle of Gigha in the Hebrides talks about how the service was used by the locals to send animals through the post.

Royal Mail • Post Office workers at the Mount Pleasant sorting office in London in 1964 getting mail ready to be delivered.

▼

TIMELINE

1949	The horse-drawn mail van is used for the last time in London
1959	Modern postcodes are used for the first time in Britain
1962	Modpeds are used for postal delivery as a trial
1968	1st and 2nd class stamps are introduced for the first time
1969	7 million working days lost to strike action
1971	The first postal strike over pay
1996	The last telegram is sent

▲

Car assembly line • *Today, manual labour such as car manufacturing, is aided with computer technology and even robots.*

Delivery to homes accounts for one in every ten items of post. Over 190,000 people are employed in a great variety of jobs and there are over 14,000 Post Office branches nationwide. The business does not only involve collecting, sorting and delivering mail in the UK and elsewhere. It has changed to offer banking and financial services, insurance policies and **mortgages**.

Making Cars

Car manufacturing suffered a similar fate to that of mining. In the 1940s and 1950s, the British car industry was thriving. The Morris Minor became the first British car to reach one million sales. The car was made for the first time in 1959 and struck a cord with the cultural scene of the swinging sixties. It became the car of choice for pop stars and royalty alike. In 1965, nearly all the cars bought in Britain were also made here.

However, industrial unrest and strikes amongst workers in car plants led to a downward spiral in the industry. A mere 15 years later, under half of all new cars bought were made in this country. Management disputes with workers led to accusations of the cars being poorly put together. The public lost faith in British-made cars. Today, the new mini has made a comeback and is still built in Britain, but it is now owned by the German company, BMW.

Working in the NHS

The National Health Service (NHS) was brought into existence by the Labour government after the Second World War. It was formed on 5th July, 1948, and was soon to become one of the biggest employers in the world. In 1949, it had fewer than 12,000 people working for it. Today, it employs over one million people and has a budget paid for by the **tax system** of over £42 billion. Workers include general practitioners (GPs), surgeons, consultants, anaesthetists, nurses, hospital porters, caterers, teaching staff, accountants, paramedics, **chaplains**, physiotherapists and opticians.

On the wards • *Nurses from overseas filled a huge gap in the National Health Service and provided a vital service for years to come. This nurse is looking after a patient in the 1970s.*

Too Many Vacancies

The NHS became very popular and had to expand quickly. In the 1950s, there were not enough people in Britain with the right qualifications to fill all the vacancies that were appearing. A recruitment team was sent to the Caribbean to see if they could find qualified nurses to come to Britain. Those that did make the journey were given the right to stay in 1962.

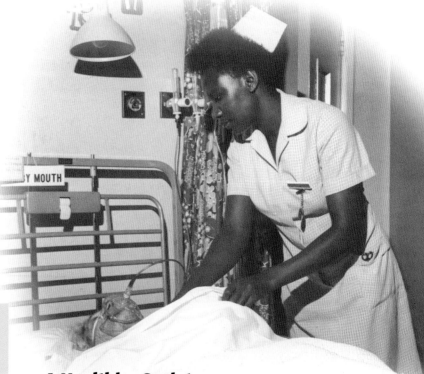

A Healthier Society

The NHS was not only a huge employer. It also helped the rest of the working population by slowly making it healthier. Diseases such as **polio** and **tuberculosis** crippled and even killed many people in Britain in the first half of the twentieth century. **Vaccines** for polio were developed in the 1950s and early 1960s and were given to the population by lots of nurses.

TIMELINE

1948	Birth of the National Health Service
1952	London smog, caused by pollution and fog, kills thousands
1960	Oral contraception available in family planning clinics for the first time
1965	Tobacco advertising ban on television
1978	The first test-tube baby in the world is born in Oldham, England
1981	The first case of AIDS is reported
1988	MMR vaccine introduced
1997	Dolly the Sheep becomes the first cloned mammal

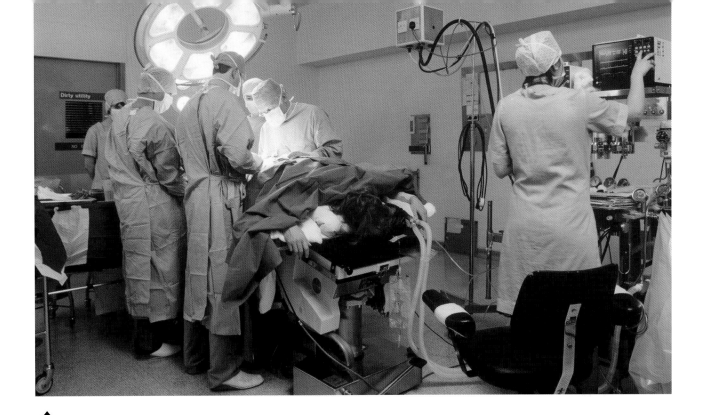

▲

Hospitals today • An operating theatre in a hospital today. It contains millions of pounds worth of equipment, delivering anaesthetic to patients as well monitoring their heart, lungs and brain functions.

This gradually stamped out the disease. The vaccine for tuberculosis had been around since the early twentieth century, but mass vaccination did not take place until after the Second World War. The disease once accounted for one in every eight deaths in this country.

In 1988, the measles, mumps and rubella (MMR) vaccination was developed and given to children in the UK with the aim of getting rid of these diseases. In surgery, new short-acting anaesthetics meant that patients recovered more quickly from operations with few side-effects. These developments in anaesthetic meant that in some cases, people could have surgery and go home the same day.

INVESTIGATE

A day in the life of the NHS

Over 835,000 people will go to their local doctor or nurse

50,000 will go to the Accident and Emergency (A&E) departments of their nearest hospital

Almost 100,000 people will be admitted into hospital as emergency patients

28,000 people will have an eyesight test

18,000 people will make a call to NHS Direct for advice on an illness or medical condition

▶ **Can you find out how many people visit your local hospital every day?**

Then in 1998, NHS Direct was introduced allowing people to talk to specialists over the phone. Within a very short space of time it was handling 500,000 calls or more a month. The drive to bring down waiting time for patients needing operations has been a priority in the twenty-first century.

The Rise of Advertising and the Media

Wages increased in the 1950s and 1960s, giving people more spending power. Technology became increasingly important in people's lives, providing more and more goods for them to buy such as televisions (48,000 sets in 1948 rising to nearly 1.5 million by 1952), cars and motorbikes, washing machines, fridges and holidays.

Seeing Opportunities

As these developments took place, so opportunities to advertise these goods to an increasingly well-off society arose. Along with this, came the spread of the media into people's lives via radio, BBC television and then commercial television in the mid 1950s, newspapers and magazines. Jobs were being created for a whole new industry – advertising in the media.

▲ **Christian Dior** • *A magazine advert selling women's lipstick. It uses women's desire to be beautiful to help sell the product.*

It was the job of advertising to find markets for all these goods by selling the idea of a different lifestyle, using the new forms of the media. It is something we are very familiar with today. Indeed advertising has been around since the Victorian era. What the combination of media (such as television and magazines) did was to bring advertising into people's homes to an intensity never seen before.

Advertising as a Growth Industry

All the big companies saw the power advertising had to market their goods. In fact, this had started in the 1930s in America, where the advertising agency was born. People were learning how to package and brand their goods. Eventually the techniques they used were taken up even by politicians and political parties.

Today, advertising is part of our everyday lives. We see and hear it everywhere – on billboards throughout our towns and cities, as pop-ups on our computers, on the television, via our mobile phones, on the radio, and pushed through our letter boxes. All businesses in the modern world, large or small, use multiple forms of the media to sell us products. In 2006, over £19 billion was spent in the UK on advertising.

In 2007, advertising budgets in most British companies increased more than they had done for the past seven years taking this figure to well over £20 billion.

The Media

Books, newspapers, magazines, television, radio, film and the internet are all forms of the media. Through them people communicate, advertise and sell. This industry has grown rapidly from 1948 up to the present day. This is because our appetite to get news, read stories, and be shown the latest product to buy has grown.

CHANGING TIMES

In the 1950s, a manufacturer with lots of money and a powerful product to market, could sponsor a programme on television. For example, there was the Colgate Comedy Hour (Colgate did and still do make toothbrushes and toothpaste).

The Profumo Affair • *The power of the newspaper industry was huge in the 1960s. The scandal in the government of the day, known as the Profumo affair, was front page news.*

Music and Publishing

Music is another area of human activity in which the combination of new media, such as radio and television, combined with increased wealth in Britain through the 1950s and 1960s, transformed it into a boom industry.

The Birth of Rock and Roll

The music industry was further vitalised by the birth of rock and roll and pop music, together with the arrival of youth culture in the 1960s. Suddenly a new market began to open up on a vast scale. Record labels, such as HMV and Decca began producing stars such as the American rock and roll singer Elvis Presley. British stars such as Cliff Richard copied his style and their music became popular all over Britain.

The King • *Elvis Presley was not only a Rock and Roll star. He was also a successful actor. Here he is playing the guitar in the 1957 film* Loving You.

 INVESTIGATE The very first pop chart was announced in Britain in 1952. Here are the top ten from that chart:

No.	Artist	Song title
1	Al Martino	Here in my heart
2	Jo Stafford	You belong to me
3	Nat King Cole	Somewhere along the way
4	Bing Crosby	Isle of Innisfree
5	Guy Mitchell	Feet up
6	Rosemary Clooney	Half as much
7	Vera Lynn	Forget me not
8	Frankie Laine	High Noon
9	Doris Day and Frankie Laine	Sugarbush
10	Ray Martin	Blue Tango

▶ **Can you find out what single was at number one in the week you were born?**

TIMELINE

1952	First pop chart in Britain
1985	The Beatles are estimated to have sold 1 billion records, discs and tapes worldwide
1997	The first Harry Potter title is published; *Harry Potter and the Philosopher's Stone*
2001	The first *Lord of the Rings* title is released as a film, *The Fellowship of the Ring*

SOUNDBITES

Radio Caroline first went out over the air at Easter in 1964. It was called a pirate radio station because it broadcast out in the sea, where it was difficult to be closed down. Both the Rolling Stones and the Beatles played live on the radio's first show.

Book Publishing

Books and newspapers have been part of our culture and society for hundreds of years, with magazines making a later entry. Today, more new book titles are being published and bought than ever before.

By the end of the twentieth century, publishing was estimated to be worth about £18.5 billion and employed over 140,000 people. People in this country spent almost £2.5 billion on books, £2.7 billion on newspapers and £1.2 billion on magazines in 1999. Children's book publishing has been one area of great success in recent years. For example in 2007, *Harry Potter and the Deathly Hallows* sold 2.5 million copies in the first 24 hours of being on sale, breaking all previous records.

Tourism and Leisure

Before the Second World War, more than 10 million people would go on holiday each year but most would holiday in Britain. The tourism industry barely existed in 1948, and people did not have the money or the means to go far. Commercial airlines as we know them did not exist and far fewer people owned cars. The railways had just been nationalised by the Labour party and were being repaired after five years of war. Britain did have plenty of seaside resorts but it would take a few years for the economy to recover enough for people to go back to them in any numbers.

Advertising • *A typical early advert from the 1960s selling the sun and sandy beaches of the Spanish Mediterranean coast.*

The Rise of the Package Holiday

This was all to change. Very quickly after the Second World War, aircraft were used to fly passengers around Europe to destinations such as Paris, London and Rome. Air fares were expensive by today's standards. Then came the breakthrough with package holidays. One company would provide transport, accommodation and meals at a holiday resort for an affordable amount. Corsica was the very first destination, in 1950. Spain very quickly became popular with British holiday-makers. Resorts on the Costa del Sol and the Costa Blanca sprang up to cater for their needs.

Welcome to a holiday you'll never forget—to the thrill of hot sand beneath your feet—to the lazy murmur of the blue, blue Mediterranean— to the golden glory of sun-drenched beaches, gently fanned by princely palms. Welcome, welcome to Spain.

This year...next year...sometime...ever

SPAIN

See your travel agent for full information

Air travel • *British Airways staff photographed in their new uniforms in 1994. Air travel from the UK was increasing every year as flights became cheaper.*

Tourism in Spain:
Spain has been the most popular destination for tourists in Europe since the 1960s. Nearly all visitors (almost nine out of 10) come from other European countries, and Britain is high on the list.

Year	Number of tourists in Spain
1960	6 million
1970	24 million
1980	38 million
1990	55 million
2001	50 million

A Whole New Industry

Very soon a whole range of jobs were created to service this now growing industry – holiday reps, travel agents, civil airline pilots and their crew. By the 1960s, foreign holidays were seen by the majority of people in Britain as part of the modern lifestyle, along with owning a car, a television and a fridge. Through the power of advertising, people were more aware of them than ever before. Those that could not afford to go abroad stayed at home, mostly heading for the seaside, or to the mountains of the Lake District and Snowdonia which are both National Parks.

All of a sudden, holiday destinations were in competition with each other over the increasingly **profitable** holiday maker. Today, millions of people from this country go abroad for their holidays. However, it is estimated that over 100 million tourist visits are made to National Parks in England and Wales each year.

The Specialist Holiday

In recent years, tourism has started to cater for specialist holidays – family holidays to Disney World in America, diving holidays on the Red Sea in Israel and sailing the Greek islands. There are also holidays for specific age groups – for example, Club 18-30 or Saga holidays for those over 50. From 2007, there is even space tourism for the super-rich. Passengers can now orbit around the Earth for a £15 million fare!

The Armed Forces

The Armed Forces make up the Navy, the Air Force and the Army. Together they employ a total of 294,000 people, including 100,000 who have civilian roles. Jobs include frontline infantry, fighter pilots, helicopter pilots, special forces, medical personnel, caterers, engineers, communications staff, career advisors, office workers and public relations experts.

Technology and the Armed Forces

As with so much in modern times, jobs in the Armed Forces have become more specialised and demand more qualifications and training than they did in 1948. Fighting equipment in all three of the Armed Forces has changed considerably in this time as well. Technological advances in weaponry have given the soldier, sailor and pilot laser-guided bullets and missiles, **supersonic** jets, night-vision visors, **Kevlar** vests and satellite communications.

This is all a long way from the relatively simple though very effective design of the **Spitfire aircraft**, the battleships and the **Bren gun** of the British soldier in the Second World War.

▲
The Korean War • *British soldiers and their captain in Korea in 1951 during the war with the Communist regime.*

A Drop in Numbers

The Armed Forces have declined in the number of people employed over the last six decades. Since 1994 for example, the number of military personnel has been cut by around 20%. This is partly to do with the fact that since the Second World War there has not been the need to have a large Armed Force. Technology has also played a role. Modern weaponry has replaced the need to have lots of soldiers on a battlefield, for example.

TIMELINE

1945	About 4.5 million people in the Armed Forces immediately following the end of the Second World War. The highest number there had ever been
1950-53	The Korean War
1990	487,000 are employed by the UK Armed Forces. This is reduced to 294,000 by 2007
2006-7	UK Armed Forces spend £11,672,000,000 on equipment

▲
Military work • *Inside the cockpit with the pilots of an RAF Sea King helicopter as it flies on a practice run over the English Lake District.*

It is expensive for a country to keep a large Army and so there is a need to keep numbers to a minimum. In 1964, the Ministry of Defence was formed out of the three governing bodies – the Admiralty (Navy), the War Office (Army), and the Air Ministry (Airforce). Reporting to the MoD are five Chiefs of Staff, including the head of the Army, called the Chief of the General Staff, the Chief of the Air Staff, and the Chief of the Naval Staff.

Voices from history

Many of the men who fought in the Second World War were not soldiers when it began. They joined up during the war, having had other jobs previously. Here is one first-hand account of the end of the war and getting back to normal life in Britain in the late 1940s:

'At the end of World War II, I returned to the UK being **demobbed** and went back to Liverpool, thankful to be home safe, and to be with my wife and child, who was born while I was away at war. Liverpool to my eyes, looked a great place, as I got my old job back on the docks. I stayed here for the rest of my life.'

From the letters of a Second World War soldier from the BBC website.

Working at the Cutting Edge

Of all the professions that have changed the face of the modern world since 1948, that of the scientist and the engineer must have had the biggest impact. Science has lead a technological revolution that has reached into every aspect of our lives – health, medicine and hygiene, textiles, transport, energy, warfare, food, communications and nearly all our workplaces.

Research and Development

Scientists now have places on government committees and in big businesses. For example, companies, such as ICI, set up establishments in the 1950s and 1960s, to research detergents for cleaning our homes and chemicals to help farmers fight pests.

These research establishments have grown over the last six decades, to become a vital part of drugs companies, textile manufacturers, computer software design firms and genetically modified food corporations. Research and development, as it is called, makes up a large part of the cost of running many businesses today. These companies spend enormous sums of money looking at new drugs to help prevent or cure diseases, make our computers function more quickly and efficiently and help us communicate more easily. Increasingly they are looking for ways to help us power our world with less energy or energy from **renewable sources**, such as the sun, wind and waves.

ICI • Founded in 1926, ICI stands for Imperial Chemicals Industries. In 2006, it employed 26,000 people and had £4.8 billion in sales. In 2007, the British company announced it had been bought by the Dutch Akzo Nobel.

TIMELINE

1958	The first microchip is manufactured
1969	Computers are first linked to each other to form a mini-internet
1983	300,000 full-time UK students are in higher education, the highest figure up to that point
2003	The human **genome** is decoded and available for science
2006	ICI employs 26,000 people and has an annual sale of £4.8 billion

Voices from history

'Research represents the lifeblood of the University... It powers everything we do, from our innovative teaching methods to our growing portfolio of spin out companies.

Without research we simply would not be able to teach in the way we do... our students learn from world leaders in their fields, from the pioneers of the World Wide Web to the leaders of ocean and earth sciences, from world-renowned marine engineers to prominent medical professionals.'

One higher institution describes the cutting-edge research that is done at universities in the twenty first century.

▲

Education plays a part • University chemistry students attend a class on the structure of molecules.

The Role of Universities

The growth in university places in the 1960s and 1970s, along with the development of polytechnics, fed the need for more scientists and engineers in the workplace. The future of Britain in a global market lies increasingly in the hands of those who find solutions to technological problems. Today, a great deal of time and money is spent on researching sources of energy that can keep the world developing but with less pollution and dependence on fossil fuels such as oil, coal and gas.

Working for Yourself

In the early twenty-first century, one in ten working people were self-employed. Being self-employed can take the form of setting up your own business and employing other people or hiring out your services to many different companies. However, changes in the workplace and technological advances have made it easier to be self-employed than ever before. Many people choose to work from home, rather than be a commuter travelling long distances to work.

The Aid of the Computer

Computers at home and in the workplace, along with broadband access to the internet, have made communications far easier and faster than they were even a few years ago. Now large files containing millions of words, colour photographs and artwork can be sent all around the country and abroad from a worker at home to businesses in seconds. Many businesses today would rather hire in work help as they need it from freelancers rather than pay for full-time staff. The era of having the same job for life has disappeared.

Working from home •
This woman is working from her office at home. Advances in technology means she can have a video conference call to another office.

CHANGING TIMES

Back in 1948, a computer that filled a room could do about 5,000 calculations a second. Today, the most powerful computer on earth, the IBM BlueGene/L, can do 1000 trillion calculations a second!

A Change in Attitude

In the 1950s, it would have brought great shame upon someone to have their business declared **bankrupt**. The attitude to a business failing has changed considerably. Today, there is more of a climate in which people are encouraged to be ambitious. Banks, for example, will lend more money than was usually possible for past generations. But many small businesses do fail, especially in the first crucial year or two. Cash flow is generally the biggest problem. This is the balance between spending money to make the business work and getting in money from people you have done work for. If your clients pay their bills late, you may not have enough money to pay those that have done work or supplied goods for you.

Help from the Government

Another significant difference between 50 years ago and today is the amount of help people can receive from the government to help them set up a business of their own or to become self-employed. There is advice on what type of business to set up, how to pay tax, how to borrow money, and how to manage your accounts. The construction industry is an area in which many people are self-employed. Many individual companies might work on one site putting up lots of houses for example. These would include architects, engineers, bricklayers, plumbers, carpenters, roofers, and heavy plant operators.

The government can give advice to each type of profession, a resource unavailable to our grandparents. A big period of growth in self-employment came between 1986 and 1990. The government directly influenced this by introducing the small business start-up scheme. Relatively high unemployment at the time meant more people chose to set up on their own in some cases.

Timeline *Highlights in the History of Britain since 1948*

1947–1948 Britain experiences what turned out to be its coldest winter of the century

1948 The Olympic Games are held in London, called the 'Austerity Games'

1948 The railways are nationalised

July 1948 Post war Labour government unveils the National Health Service (NHS)

1951 The Festival of Britain

1952 Elizabeth II becomes Queen

1954 Post war rationing stops

1955 Commercial television starts in Britain – ITV

1958 The first stretch of motorway is opened in Britain (it forms part of what is today the M6)

1959 Conservative Prime Minister, Harold Macmillan tells the country, 'Most of our people have never had it so good'

1960 Britain seeks entry into the European Economic Community (EEC)

1965 The Post Office Tower is opened in London – the tallest, most expensive building in Britain at the time

1969 7 million working days lost to strike action

1972 Britain joins the European Economic Community (EEC)

1973 The oil crisis spells the end of cheap fuel and energy

1973 Power cuts hit the nation

1979 Margaret Thatcher becomes the first British woman Prime Minister

1982 The Falklands War

1985 The Miners' Strike

1987 London Stock Market crash – Black Monday

1998 12% of the working population are self-employed

2001 In February, Foot and Mouth disease breaks out in British farms, closing the countryside down for months and losing millions of pounds in lost tourism

2006 Over £19 billion spent on advertising in the UK

2006-7 UK Armed Forces spend £11,672,000,000 on equipment

Glossary

'Austerity Britain' The period (1945 – 1951) after the Second World War when rationing in food and clothes meant the population was under-fed and queued for basic items

bankrupt A business or company that runs out of money and can no longer carry out its trade

Bren gun A quick firing machine gun used by the allied forces in the Second World War

chaplain Someone from the church who is attached to a non-religious organisation, like the army or a hospital

colonies Countries or areas under the political rule of another country

demobbed A soldier coming home from war and leaving the army was said to be demobbed

economy A system in which a country organises the production of goods and services

genome The human genetic make-up

import Something that is brought into the country having been grown or made abroad

Kevlar A man-made fibre invented in the 1960s. It is five times stronger than steel and is used as body armour

manufacturing The process of making goods, either by hand or in a factory system

mortgage A special loan from a bank or building society for the purpose of buying a house or similar property

National Parks Areas in the UK that are thought to be of special landscape value and therefore need protection

nationalise To take out of private ownership and make the property of the nation as a whole

polio An illness that causes inflammation in the spine and can lead to disability

profitable A business that makes money is said to be profitable. Making a profit is the key to running a successful company

rationing The process by which food and clothing are made available to people to buy on a limited basis due to shortage

renewable source an energy source that can be reused

Spitfire aircraft A fighter plane in the British airforce during the Second World War. It was a single-seater plane, designed in the 1930s by R J Mitchell

supersonic Able to travel faster than the speed of sound – 1,238 kilometres per hour or 769 miles per hour

tax system A system in which the government raises money by taking it from the population

tenant farmer A farmer who rents a farm, paying money to the owner

tuberculosis A disease that causes small lumps to form in the lungs and elsewhere in the body

vaccine Medicine that is given to people to help them become immune to certain diseases

FURTHER INFORMATION

📖 Books

Britain Since World War II: Media and Entertainment Colin Hynson (Franklin Watts, 2007)

Britain Since World War II: Work and Industry Jim Bruce (Franklin Watts, 2007)

The History Detective Investigates: Post-war Britain Simon Adams (Wayland, 2008)

In the War: Food and Rations Peter Hicks (Wayland, 2008)

In the War: School Life Peter Hicks (Wayland, 2008)

🖱 Websites

http://www.postalheritage.org
Look back to the spectacular History of the Post Office

http://www.networkrail.co.uk
Check out the plans for the our railways in the twenty-first century

http://www.bbc.co.uk/schools
Find out about life in Britain throughout history

http://www.nhshistory.net
Investigate the history of the NHS

http://www.hfusc.org.uk
This website has many personal voices from history and lots of resources to investigate the changes that have happened in Britain since 1948

Index

Numbers in **bold** refer to photographs.

BRITAIN SINCE 1948

Contents of titles in the series:

WAYLAND